W7-BNR-074

D0117886

SUITS ON...
GAME ON...
Know Your Position!

CHRIS HAYES
Super Bowl Champ to some...
                    Mentor to many!

3030hayes @ gmail.com

Www. mygameclip.com

(cell) 818 - 381 - 2141

SUITS ON... GAME ON... *Know Your Position!*

Published by:

Copyright © 2007 by Chris Hayes

All rights reserved. No part of this book may be reproduced in any form, except for the inclusion of brief quotations in a review, without permission in writing from the author and publisher.

ISBN: 978-1-60461-818-1
Library of Congress Control Number: 2007908213

To book Chris Hayes for a sports camp, speaking engagement, fundraising or community event please contact
3030hayes@gmail.com.

Printed in the United States by:
Morris Publishing
3212 East Highway 30
Kearney, NE 68847
1-800-650-7888

TABLE OF CONTENTS

Dear Champions,

This book provides motivational strategies that you can reference daily. It is an interactive book created to help you achieve your goals in business by utilizing footballs plays to develop a strategic path for success. The tactics in this book describe how to break down business maneuvers in the same manner you might break down the success of an all-star sports team. This book provides an outline to make it easier to understand the way the game works and to also dissect the formidable opponents and varying playing fields that you will encounter in business. Take the time to use the space provided to outline your own business plays as well as review your past wins and losses.

Winning teams are made up of players who are 100 percent committed to the play. They're willing to put in hard work with a positive attitude, and they're ready to define each play's criteria to build the team accordingly. Remember, games are won by gaining yards and consistently moving the ball forward. Business deals are closed in the exact same manner. If you drop the ball, pick it up and run again.

If you have the time, sit down and give this playbook a good long read. Or, if you're like most people and have little time, carry the book with you and flip through the pages. You can open this book to any page, at any time, and find something to inspire you, enlighten you, or make your day more productive.

My hope is that when you finish this book, you will have added so many of your own victories that this book will become a daily tool for the continued growth of your business and success of your career. This will give you the opportunity to reflect on the thoughts, challenges, and skill development you used to triumph. Utilize this guide to help you realize your champion within like I continue to know mine... I hope you enjoy reading this book as much as I enjoy sharing it.

Peace,

Chris "Peto" Hayes

Acknowledgements:

First, I would like to give thanks to my Lord and Savior, Jesus Christ. Who am I but what you allow me to be. Father, I ask that you continue to use me. Father, expand my territory so that your message is delivered to the proper audiences.

I would like to give thanks to my caring, loving, and supportive wife, Aran. You are my true homie, lover, and friend. You have shown unbelievable patience for me and for my pursuit of this dream for the past 14 years. Words cannot describe the love I have for you. Without you, none of this could have been possible.

I would like to give thanks to my three sons, Chris Jr., Isaiah, and Jeremiah "JJ" Hayes, for all the love they show Daddy on a daily basis. I pray that the Lord continues to bless each one of you. I could not ask for better sons than I have. Daddy and Mommy are proud of you.

I would like to give thanks to Mom and Pop for all of their love and support. Big Hayes, thanks for keeping me active and out of trouble. I thank God for such a beautiful family. Mom, you are definitely a strong black woman, who simultaneously held us down and raised us up. I would like to thank all my brothers and sisters for all the memories we have…and all the battles we have fought together.

I would like to thank Mrs. Jill D'Andrea for co-authoring this book with me. Jill, you are amazing. The way you were able to capture everything and bring it to life is phenomenal. You are definitely a team player. The only thing missing is your Super Bowl-sized ring. Thanks a million copies sold…

I would like to thank Renae for riding in the passenger seat since the early 1990s. I know you did not want any love in the acknowledgements, but how could I leave you out? This is just the beginning. It's about time that we can finally share our vision with people.

I would like to give thanks to my brothers in Christ, Minister Briggs and Robert Newt. Thanks for having my back when I felt the world turned its back on me. Each of you has been such a blessing for my family and for me. The talent and the vision are crazy. I cannot wait 'til they can hear your music. I cannot forget my sistas and nephew. Thank you, Endya, Courtney "Red Bone," and Prince Judah.

I would like to thank my fraternity, Phi Beta Sigma, Blue Phi. Reverend Dr. Bennie Harris, Terrell Henderson, Greg Burns, Santana Lewis, Leon Strayer, Justin Stallins, Derek Sparks, and Leon "LB" Bender; I miss you, frat. Young Christopher Johnson, man, let's take this thing to the next level. Your books are going to change up the game. Continue to trust in the Lord and lean not on your own understanding.

I would like to thank Keyshawn Johnson for all the support. Keep doing your thing, representing on ESPN. I know this book isn't like your book, "Throw Me the Damn Ball," but I am using a similar format. I am taking this one straight to the field.

I would like to thank my business partner, Terrance "T-Luc" Lucas, for supporting me since the Green Bay Packers days. I am proud of you and your family. I have seen you grow up over the years and it has been a blessing. Continue to be the husband that God has called you forth to be and the father you have been ordained to be. God bless you and your family.

I would like to thank everyone that is involved with the 3030 Foundation. Principal Sandra Rodriquez, you are God's gift to San Bernardino School District. Pastor Willie, thanks for showing us love. God bless you and your congregation. I would also like to thank Shawn Battle of the SBPD for always keeping it real. Loved ones, be safe out there protecting our community.

Thanks and Love to everyone for praying and believing in me... I hope you all enjoy.

Chris "Peto" Hayes

WHY ME?

You may be asking why I wrote a book like this. It is not because I am an eight-year NFL veteran with a Super Bowl ring. It is not because I played as an under-sized linebacker for one of the most dominating defenses in the Pac-10. It is not because I played for three NFL teams in a one-year span. No. It's because I'm just like you: someone who had to struggle to find the champion within.

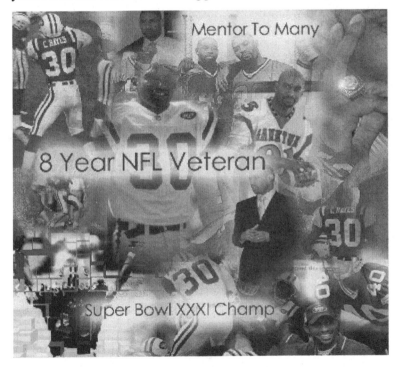

You know the story: I came from a tough neighborhood, I was given the shot of a lifetime, and I became part of a multi-billion dollar enterprise. I had money, success, and opportunity for the taking. But what you might not know is how *hard* I had to work to get where I am today, both financially and spiritually.

It's true: I was given incredible physical gifts that allowed me to rise above a situation that could have swallowed me whole. Football was my ticket out. But I'll tell you this: nothing was handed to me. I had to work. I had to fight. I had to face adversity just like everyone else—just like you. In the NFL, I was cut, signed, cut, signed, cut again. I was told I wasn't good enough, wasn't fast enough. But I refused to give up. I knew what I wanted, and I knew it wasn't going to be easy, and I always found myself in a struggle. I couldn't understand why life had to be so difficult. No matter what I had or didn't have, no matter what I was able to achieve or not achieve, I always found myself battling to work it out. Why couldn't life just be…easier? Because I didn't have a plan. Because I didn't have a *playbook for life.*

Once I realized that the strategies, attitudes, tendencies, and plays I used on the gridiron could be applied to the rest of my life, I found success. And not just with football, but with my business, my family, and my relationship with God.

I'm no different from you. I understand what it's like to work hard and dream big. I'm here to help you unlock that champion within. No matter what you choose to do in your life—corporate executive, extraordinary teacher, proud parent, loving spouse—you *can* achieve it. Just follow the playbook…

I have spent the better part of my post-NFL career trying to give back to the individuals and the communities that have inspired me to dream bigger, work harder, and achieve greater. I established 30THIRTY, a non-profit organization dedicated to enriching the lives of children and teens who might otherwise fall through the ever-widening cracks. Find out how to get involved and make a difference in a child's life at **30thirtyhayes.com**. Because ultimately, success is not measured by how much you have, but by how much you share.

THE BASIC FUNDAMENTALS

First off, you have to know who you are. Before you can call yourself a team player, you have to know what you're willing to do to win the game. Whether it's the game of football, the game of corporate America, or the game of life—it doesn't matter. Who are you?

What kind of player are you?
How hard are you willing to work?
What sacrifices are you willing to make?

TEAM PLAYER

You know the saying: "There's no 'I' in team." Well, that might not be entirely true. Great corporations, like championship sports teams, are built on the concept of teamwork. But within the team structure, there are individuals whose talents and accomplishments we celebrate. Michael Jordan may be an exceptional team player, but when you think of the Chicago Bulls, you think, "Michael Jordan." This is because he stood out as an individual, because he had the talent, the drive, and the determination to shine. As a result, he received well-deserved personal accolades. But, on the other hand, Michael Jordan would have no place to showcase his talents if it weren't for the Chicago Bulls or the NBA. In other words, someone has to pass you the ball...but only *you* can decide how to run with it.

Personal success and teamwork don't have to be exclusive of each other. Teams are made up of individuals. A leader is an integral part of the team, but leaders are also individuals. Each player has a specific responsibility—as an individual—to live up to his or her obligation to the team. You should always keep in mind that as an individual, you are responsible for supporting, inspiring, and motivating your team, whether it's a sports team, a corporate team, or even your family. Everyone on the team has the same goal—to get the ball over the goal line. But if you really want to succeed, you need to step forward. You need to take ownership of your work, your mission, your project, or your game.

Striving for your own personal success should not be confused with parading your own personal ego. No one ever succeeds alone. There's always someone to thank, someone to dedicate your success to. Personal achievements should always be re-directed toward the greater goal, the team goal. In business, you might have a great idea, something so innovative it could revolutionize your business. Presenting your findings to the world might bring you international recognition. But in the end, your company, your clients, or the world in general will reap the benefits as well. Team success is driven by individual achievement. You can't have the former without the latter.

COMMITMENT

So, are you a team player? Of course you are. Now you need to decide which position you want to play. Are you going to be a linebacker? If you are, you have to be prepared for whatever gets thrown at you. Are you going to be the quarterback? If you are, you have to be swift on your feet and make quick, accurate decisions. Are you going to be the top sales rep for your region? If you are, you have to build a solid client base and sell your product—better than anyone else. Are you going to be the best spouse, parent, son, or daughter that you can be? If you are, you have to love, support, tolerate, and forgive on a daily basis. But most of all, you have to get off the bench and get into the game.

Committing to a position doesn't mean you're stuck there for the rest of your life. Not at all. One of the first things I learned when I signed with the NFL was that "**NFL** also stands for **N**ot **F**or **L**ong." The average NFL career is 2–4 years. This means that the average player will have to make the bulk of his lifetime earnings, professional contacts, and future career opportunities in 2–4 years. Not much time for error. The game of football, like the game of life, is always changing. Every day, when you enter the field (your office), there are 30 kids younger, stronger, and better educated—all of them just itching to take your job. Those of you who beat the odds will get up every morning, get dressed, and decide that today you will succeed, today you will survive. Today you will be committed to the game in front of you.

The game of football, like the game of life, is always changing. The demands of the game are never the same from season to season, game to game, or even quarter to quarter. So go ahead and commit to that position, but don't count on playing there for the rest of your life. The day you sign a contract, whether it's with a mortgage banking company or with the NFL, there's only one thing for certain: one day your services will no longer be needed. That's the only guarantee. So make the most of it while you can. Change is good. But in order to do the best job you can for the time you're in the game, you must commit. All the way.

A STRONG FOUNDATION

Every position has its responsibilities, and every player must know what's expected. This is where the basic fundamentals come into play. This is where you build your foundation. When you entered your profession, there was a knowledge and skill base that you were expected to learn and master. These are the things you'll always come back to. How do you build a client base? How do you network? How do you close the deal? When I came to the NFL, I was always coming back to my first up/down, my first pursuit angle, or my first tackle. They were strategies I learned in high school that stuck with me throughout my NFL career, because they defined my training experience, the molding of my skills and tendencies—the basic fundamentals.

You'll always come back to how you were trained. Simplify it, adapt it, and apply it. In the business world, this translates to having the right materials and the right instructions. For instance, when you're a new account executive, they give you the guidelines, the matrices, and the rate sheets—things you have to study. They form the foundation of the job and you must know them. So, corporate America basically hands you the infrastructure—the guidelines of that company—and you build on that. What's your company's platform? What do they specialize in? Do they have a niche? What are the principles that drive this company? You have to know all these things in order to grow and excel. Without the foundation, you have no game.

And don't think you need to be right out of college or fresh on the job to make this play work. You can re-examine the basic fundamentals at any point in your career. Sometimes you just need to be reminded of the things you already know. Sometimes you're learning all this like it's new because you didn't pay attention the first time around. That's okay—your head is in the game now, and that's all that counts.

Think of a pyramid. The pyramids in Egypt were built on strong foundations—therefore, they withstood the test of time. The bottom level of the pyramid is the biggest and strongest layer—it supports the entire structure. The same principles apply to any kind of life situation, whether it's football, business, or even spirituality. If you're a spiritual person, God is at the base of your pyramid, and everything else rests on His powerful shoulders. Now take that idea to corporate America. Give yourself a foundation of knowledge and skill that supports the kind of success you desire.

MAKE YOUR PLAYS...

In the back of this book, there are sample football plays with descriptions of when you might want to apply them. Use the blank work sections at the end of each chapter to create some plays that might apply to deals you're working on right now. Below is a sample that illustrates a short yardage play. You might apply this play to begin negotiations on a new deal or to close a deal. No matter how you use the play, don't start the game without a plan.

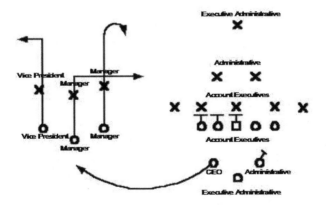

GOAL
CLOSE THE DEAL

PLAY ON...

POST GAME REVIEW...

In these sections, use the blank pages to review your wins and losses in conjunction with what you have learned in the chapter. Take this opportunity to write out lessons learned or to highlight great successes. Goals are achieved after several tackles, so think about the times you found an opening and how you used it to your advantage. Study your failures to learn from your weaknesses and study your triumphs to build on your strengths.

WINS AND LOSSES...

PREPARATION—
THE WARM-UP:

The legendary basketball coach John Wooden once said, "Failing to prepare is preparing to fail." Preparation is one of the most important elements to a successful career. After you understand the basic fundamentals and have built a solid foundation, you can apply your knowledge and use your skills to develop a plan. A great plan requires goals, objectives, and vision. What is your personal agenda and how does it relate to the team? Are you just daydreaming, or do you have a legitimate vision? How do you manage the details of your plan? What exercises can you do to prime your business muscles? Warming up is conditioning your body to move like it's already in the game. Establish a good warm-up routine and you won't have to think about goals and objectives after the game starts—it will be automatic.

Preparation is an on-going and never-ending key to success. You don't just prepare at the beginning of the game. You continue to prepare at every juncture. Every time they blow the whistle, you re-align and make new plans. Preparation includes research, which is something you'll come back to in every quarter, on every play. Knowledge is power, and the more you know, the more likely you are to win the game. You might think you can wow your clients on-the-fly, but why take that chance when you could lose everything simply because you weren't prepared?

UNDERSTAND YOUR OPPONENT

I can't stress this enough. Who is your opponent? Anyone who isn't on your team... *yet*. Understanding your opponent means figuring out exactly how they operate. If you're able to walk in their shoes, you'll be able to predict their moves. But this only works if you maintain control—and a level head. Emotions do not belong in the board room. Fortunately for you, not everybody recognizes this key principle. Understanding your opponent's emotional involvement—or better yet, their emotional *tendencies*—will keep you one step ahead of the game.

You often hear how important it is to make a good first impression. This is because, by and large, people are simple creatures. They operate on feelings and emotions, and they make judgments accordingly. There may be thousands of men and women selling the same thing you're selling or pitching the same great idea. There may be thousands of people in your position who can do the same quality of work. So if your boss, or a potential client, can get the same service, quality, and product from ten different people, it all boils down to one thing. Who makes the best impression? Who do they like the most? Who makes them *feel* the best about a potential working relationship? This is simple human nature. Everyone wants to have a positive experience, especially at work where attitude can dictate performance. Everyone wants to feel good! Your clients need to feel secure and know that the job will get done right. Your boss needs to feel safe, to believe that you're the right person to handle the project. You can say, "It's not what you know, it's who you know." Or you can chalk it up to the "law of attraction," but it all boils down to feelings and emotions. Keep yours in check. And check out everybody else's.

So how do you unearth your opponent's emotional tendencies? You can start with your computer. The Internet is an amazing resource. You can research companies, people, trends—anything you can think of. Find out as much as you can about your opponents. Use this information for your benefit. Let them know you're interested in them—not just as businesspeople, but as thinking, feeling *human* beings. Find out about their accomplishments, their philanthropy, and their hobbies. Connect with them on another level—make them *feel* like you're on their team.

GOALS

Everybody has to have goals. Goals are big ideas that explain the final outcome. The goal in football is to win the game. The goal for any team in the NFL is to win the Super Bowl. The goal for a mortgage banking company is to originate and service a certain number of loans for a targeted number of clients. The goal for a retail corporation is to sell the most products at the highest profit margin. Great. But how do we do achieve our goals? With objectives.

OBJECTIVES

Objectives are more to the point. Objectives are specific, concrete steps that are necessary to achieving that big goal. In football, you need to execute the right play to move the ball ten yards to get your first down. That's your first objective. Then you need to do that a few more times to score a touchdown. That's your second objective. You need to score more touchdowns than the other team. That's objective number three.

String these objectives together and you just won the game and achieved your ultimate goal. In business, you need to break down your goals into manageable objectives. You want to be the top executive in your company; that's a great goal. Now, what are the steps that will take you there? What are your objectives?

Stating your objectives won't make them happen. Are you willing to work hard to accomplish them? Running ten yards may sound easy on paper, but try putting on a helmet, grabbing the ball, and facing a line of guys who each weigh more than 250 pounds, and whose objective, by the way, is to keep *you* from gaining a single yard. Not so easy. To reach your goals, you have to be willing to deal with the blocks, the hits, and the tackles. You also have to know when to bob and weave. You have to know how to choose your battles, and remember: keep your ego out of the game, because that's when you get hurt.

VISION

So, you know your goals and objectives. What about the vision? This is the fun part, because you get to be creative here. Can you see yourself getting that promotion? Being in that corner office?

Visualization is a very powerful tool, because if you can't see it happening in your mind and in your heart, how can you work toward it? Professional athletes use visualization all the time. It's part of preparation. Marathon runners see themselves crossing the finish line—ahead of everyone else. Swimmers see themselves beating their personal-best time. Soccer players see the ball kicked to a spot in the corner of the net. Football players see that pass, that tackle, that interception before it happens, so they're prepared to make it actually happen.

In corporate America, you need to see yourself making that sale, pitching that idea, dominating that meeting. Go ahead and rehearse what you're going to say. You might get only one shot to impress—don't waste it because you never saw it coming. Visualization is not the same thing as daydreaming. You can sit in your cubicle fantasizing about that promotion all day—it won't make it happen. Visualization involves real, concrete steps, including creating objectives and goals for yourself. A runner sees himself crossing the finish line only after he sees himself choreographing his race. He does this by asking himself questions such as "Where am I going to push it?", "Where do I take it easy?", "When do I grab water?", and "How will the road conditions, the weather, the quality of my running shoes, my attitude, affect my performance?" You have to think of *everything* and include it in your vision, your plan, and your preparation. In the corporate world, you have to figure out what needs to be done to get that corner office, to be the top salesperson, to get that promotion.

Have you ever heard the expression "Fake it 'til you make it"? This is actually a great way to develop positive thinking. When you exude a positive attitude people want to be around you. They desire your company, your advice, and ultimately your business. When you project yourself as successful, people will believe it, and they'll feed off the energy you bring to the table. This, in turn, makes them *feel* good, which makes *them* more productive and more successful. It's the ultimate win-win situation.

EXERCISE

An easy way to organize your plan is to work backward. If you want to become a brilliant doctor, you must first go to a prestigious medical school. How do you get there? You score off-the-charts on your entrance examinations. How do you do that? You study biology and chemistry and physics as a pre-med undergraduate. How do you become a pre-med undergraduate? You study and learn by putting in the hours. Nowhere in this scenario do you get something handed to you. There are no accomplished doctors practicing today that had their degrees, or their expertise handed to them. They had to work for it, and so do you.

The path to accomplishing your goals is similar whether you want to become a doctor, an artist, or a professional hockey player. Corporate America has its own set of steps and procedures. Mapping out these steps in a logical and attainable way is a great exercise in preparing for success.

Write down your ultimate goal on a piece of paper. Let's say you want to become a district manager in your company. That's your ultimate goal. Now determine the steps you need to take to accomplish this goal. Picture each piece of the puzzle, each level of the pyramid, from the top down. What tasks actually get you the promotion to district manager? Maybe consistent sales increases in your local office and a positive formal review would be enough to get you the job. Write those tasks beneath your ultimate goal. Okay, great. What comes before that? How do you accomplish those things? What do you need to get a positive review? How do you increase sales? Write down those things; be as specific as you can, so you'll know exactly what comes next every time you cross something off the list. Picture yourself doing these things, actually going through the motions. In your vision, include scenes where you accomplish each objective, each goal. *In order.* Go ahead, write it down. Post it where you can see it, to remind yourself of each step in the process. Check off each objective as you accomplish it. Make minor adjustments to your list as needed; add tasks you overlooked and remove tasks that are no longer necessary. Eventually, you will reach your ultimate goal. Then you can decide which leather couch to put in your new office.

MAKE YOUR PLAYS...

PLAY ON...

POST GAME REVIEW...

WINS AND LOSSES...

PLAYING THE GAME:

You understand your goals and objectives, and you've spent time warming up your business moves. Now it's time to play the game. Execution is the way you carry out your objectives, the way you implement those strategies you learned through preparation, training, and exercise. Now it's time to show the team what you have to offer. In business, that means finding clients, building lasting relationships, getting on the phone, landing that meeting, and sealing that deal. You'll play many games in your career, so carry the important lessons from one game to the next. You have the mission, you have the vision—now walk it out!

1st Quarter:

Okay, it's the first quarter and you're excited to get out there and play the game! You've got your basic fundamentals in place, you know your goals and objectives, and you had a little warm-up to get you going. In football, like in business, you have a limited amount of time to make your mark. A football game is often decided by only two or three points. You're only as good as your last play, or your last phone call, or your last deal, so you have to make every moment count. You have to be prepared for anything. You could get within inches of closing that deal or making that contact, but then you blow it by the slimmest of margins. That's why you have to be prepared right from the start. Size up your opponent. And realize that life experience, like business success, like football yardage, is gained *in increments*. This means you have to set reasonable goals for every deal, for every phone call, and for every play. Once in a while, you will hit the lottery and score that 50-yard touchdown. But more often than not, you gain yards like you gain wealth, or build a client base—in increments…piece by piece and deal by deal. It takes hard work, determination, planning and a whole lot of daily motivation to stay in the battle.

OBSERVE

In the first quarter, you need to

size up your opponents, your clients, your boss, your teammates—anyone you plan to do business with. How do they move? What plays are they using?

They said I was too small, that I would never be drafted. I wasn't invited to the workouts for the guys that were supposed to be drafted, but I showed up. I studied the scouts and what they were looking for and I became that… I was drafted….

What are their tendencies? You can't beat them at their own game if you don't understand how they're playing. That's why in football, most coaches like to script out their first 10 to 15 plays to get a feel for what the opponent is up to. How do they react when I throw *this* at them? What do they do when I play *this* way? And this preparation doesn't start right before the game. It starts immediately after the game you just finished. In the NFL, Sunday is game day, but immediately after, the coaches are right back at it, breaking down film of the last game to prepare for the next game. There's no time to waste. Time is money, no matter what business you're in.

PLAN TO WORK...HARD

In football, you're only as good as your last play, and a play lasts only 10 seconds. The same idea applies to corporate America. You're only as good as your last deal, your last presentation, your last phone call. Every play counts. If you're in retail, you have to build relationships. You can't sell merchandise if you can't establish a good relationship with a potential client. Cultivate your relationships on a consistent basis. Talking to the boss about his weekend of golf or taking your client to lunch is not "brown-nosing." It's smart business. It's the process of creating a positive feeling about who you are and what you have to offer. This is putting yourself on the frontline and being an active part of the team. You have to make a good impression every day, with every meeting.

Same thing on the football field. Every play counts. You have no time to let up. You have to perform at your best, every play. You have to execute at the top of your game, using everything you've learned, every time. Sound difficult? It is. But no one ever said winning is easy. Fortunately, no one ever said winning is impossible, either.

Know this right off the bat: Nothing is easy. Nothing will be given to you. There is no big break coming, no windfall, no handout. You must understand this at the beginning of the game, in the first quarter, because winning the game depends on your hard work. There are books, seminars, get-rich-quick schemes, all designed to prey on your desire to have wealth handed to you without putting in the time and hard work. It simply doesn't work that way. Sure, you can become rich by investing wisely in the stock market or the real estate market, but only after you've taken the time to learn, prepare, and execute with vision and precision.

1996 National Football League Draft Class

MAKE YOUR PLAY...

PLAY ON...

POST GAME REVIEW...

WINS AND LOSSES...

2ND QUARTER :

You're in the game! By now, you know if it's a game you have control over or if it's a game that's going to be a challenge. You understand your opponent, you understand your obstacles, and you understand the way the other players are working and performing. If you're smart, you can make some predictions.

COMMUNICATION

The second quarter is all about learning to communicate. You need to be open and receptive to the needs of your clients and to the needs of your corporate team. Those first meetings and those first conference calls are your setup to do business, hopefully for a long and prosperous time. Don't let miscommunication, emotion, or ignorance dominate your deal. Let's say you enter into negotiations and there's somebody on the other side of the table who's immediately opposed to you. If you allow your emotions to get involved, you'll lose the deal for sure. This is when it becomes a battle of wits and you have to maintain your composure. Maybe you need to re-examine your client's needs. Maybe you need to re-examine your own expectations. Maybe you need to allow another member of your team to step up to the table to avoid a personality conflict. Even if you're the boss, you might need to step back and let another member of your team handle the deal. Remember, it's a means to an end. At the end of the day, the goal is to make the deal. When ego, pride, and emotion dictate your behavior, you lose your effectiveness. You lose the deal. Make sure your objectives are aligned and your team is on board, because no matter how you get to the goal, your aim is to *get to the goal*!

Communication is the key to sustaining those relationships you created. How are you going to service your clients? How are you going to be the guy they want to call back? The second quarter is all about concentrating on customer service and establishing a protocol for follow-ups. How are you going to be reachable? Will you carry your Blackberry, your cell phone? Will you send e-mail or just come knocking on the door to get that next meeting, that next conference call? You must have a portal plan—a simple and reliable way for people to reach you.

POSITIONING

In business, as in football, you have to be consistent and dependable. When the coach calls a play, every team member knows exactly what they have to do. Exactly. On a team, the movement and the positioning of every player is very deliberate. Everyone has a specific job to do and the success of the collective team depends on the productivity of each individual player. Same thing in corporate America. One guy can't execute the whole show; there's not enough time in the day. That's why your corporate team depends on you to perform your job to the best of your ability. This might sound like a lot of pressure and responsibility, but the truth is your *teammates* are there to clear the way for *you* to do your job. It has to work both ways to ensure success.

The second quarter is also when the coach reviews the first quarter and determines whether you are an asset to the team in this particular game. The lay of the field has been established, and the other team's tendencies have been taken into consideration. You might get replaced. You may become expendable if you're not performing up to par.

Same thing in business. If the boss comes in and tells you exactly what your numbers should be and for whatever reason you're not there, guess what? You're out of the game. Benched. On the sidelines. In business, you constantly get critiqued, assessed, replaced, reassigned, and even fired. Corporate America often has Human Resources do the dirty work. You might get a letter in the mail saying, "Your services are no longer needed." In the NFL, it was a knock on the door, "Bring your playbook, Coach wants to see you." Words you never want to hear.

But you can avoid this if you pay attention to the basic fundamentals and keep your eye on the ball. Business, like football, is a game of preparation and reaction. Always know what's going on around you if you want to maintain control of the ball.

MAKE YOUR PLAYS...

PLAY ON...

POST GAME REVIEW...

WINS AND LOSSES...

3rd Quarter:

In the third quarter, you get a new perspective and a fresh start. You just went into halftime and pulled yourself together. You evaluated your bad plays and decided how to fix them. In business, if you're not making mistakes, you're not trying hard enough. The game is always shifting, so the ability to adapt becomes a major asset. By the third quarter, you have a better understanding of the way the game is played. You may even decide it's time for a little risk.

ADAPTABILITY

In the third quarter, you have to anticipate change in the way business is done. The whole dynamic shifts. This can be good or bad. It depends on where you're sitting. Business is not static. It's dynamic. That means you have to pay attention to shifts in the framework and be prepared to bend and flex to accommodate those changes.

The third quarter gives you the opportunity to analyze your strategy. A strategy is nothing more than a dream and a plan. You have a dream so you can visualize an outcome. You have a plan so you can make that outcome a reality. Where do you want to be by the end of this quarter? This is your dream, your goal. What steps do you need to take to make it happen? This is your game plan. But to have a great strategy, you can't forget about your opponent or those obstacles that might get in your way. Good chess players don't just consider the next move, they think two, three, four, five moves in advance. To do this, they must predict what the other guy is going to do. They develop a plan for every possible combination of moves. The game changes with every move, so they must adapt their scenario to the game at hand. Same thing in business. You must plan a strategy that incorporates adaptability.

Everyone makes mistakes in their careers. It's how you manage your mistakes that counts. A real champion doesn't fold or give in to the idea that mistakes define a person. In the third quarter, you have the unique opportunity to start over. At halftime, Coach showed you what you were doing wrong. Now you can correct your mistakes. You can come out and look at the game as if the score is 0-0. You have two quarters ahead of you; time to pick up what you lost in the first two.

RISK

You cannot succeed in business or in life without taking risks. The best risks to take are those that elevate your character, your education, and your business prowess. This means you have to be willing to look like a fool if you don't know something or if you're not familiar with a procedure. Don't be afraid to lay it all on the line to better yourself. Forget about embarrassment and concentrate on opportunity. Every time you risk something, you have a potential learning experience. Be willing to get out there and learn. There are no absolute failures in life, only learning.

The bigger the risk, the bigger the payoff...and the greater the downside. You must understand what's at stake before you throw that long pass or make that phone call or present that unconventional idea to the board. Some corporate structures allow for more risk-taking than others, so it's a good idea to learn about your company's tolerance for taking chances. But even the most conservative executives are looking for that one idea, that one innovative way, to do business that no one has ever thought of before or had the guts to bring to the table. Just make sure you know what you're talking about before you call the president of the company.

Risks don't always pay off. The best risks are calculated risks, which require doing your homework. Don't fly-by-the-seat-of-your-pants. Prepare. Sometimes you need to implement your revolutionary ideas over time, rationing your risk and delivering innovation in increments. Remember: It's a marathon, not a sprint.

MAKE YOUR PLAYS...

PLAY ON...

POST GAME REVIEW...

WINS AND LOSSES...

4th Quarter:

You learned about the basic fundamentals. You trained and prepared. You walked it out to the best of your ability. You can see the goal posts. Now you have that burning desire! With knowledge and practice, that burning desire will push you through to the end. The fourth quarter is where you really get fired up, where all that you've learned is tested. The final quarter is all about pushing through. True champions never give up. They inspire others to join the fight.

DRIVE and DETERMINATION

Of all the traits an athlete can posses, drive and determination are the ones you bank on in the fourth quarter. These qualities separate excellence from mediocrity. So how do you acquire drive and determination? *By attaching meaning to your work.* Merely wanting to land that deal or get that promotion is never enough to see you through the hardships of actually getting there. There must be more to it, more at stake to make you push harder, reach higher, give all you've got. For some, their work defines them, whether it's retail, real estate, or teaching. They strive to do the best job they can and to excel in their chosen field because they choose to not settle for less. To fail would be a reflection of the bigger picture. Some honor God with their work. It doesn't matter what field you're in or what profession you choose, if you find your work meaningful, success is the only option. If you place your job, your project, or your game, within a framework of greater purpose, your intentions and actions are more meaningful, and the results will reflect that.

Drive and determination are synonymous with passion and enthusiasm, and these are the things that set the true champion apart. Why settle for mediocrity and a lack of fulfillment in your life and business when you can truly and genuinely excel? Authentic drive and determination will inevitably propel you to victory!

MAKE YOUR PLAYS...

PLAY ON...

POST GAME REVIEW...

WINS AND LOSSES...

OVERTIME:

PLAYS FOR
EVERYDAY SUCCESS

Sometimes following the game plan just isn't enough. You need more. Sometimes you need to go on the offensive, to push the limits of your effectiveness and achieve your goals. Sometimes you find yourself on the defensive, not knowing exactly what might happen next. You need to be mentally prepared for any outcome. Here are some plays to give you that quick burst of motivation when you need it the most. Whatever your situation, there's a play to help you through it.

POWER PLAY

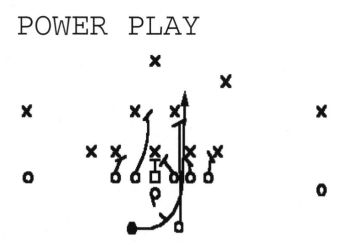

To use this play, you need ambition, confidence, and muscle. This is when you run straight-on with a powerful line. Give 'em all you've got!

AMBITION is the desire for personal advancement in your business or in your life. How badly do you want that promotion? Do you want to be given more responsibility and more freedom? Successful people are always ambitious. Unfortunately, wanting that corner office isn't enough, unless you want to be a cold, hard, friendless millionaire (and deep down I know you don't!). Ambition must be coupled with **ASPIRATION**, or the idea that what you want will lead to something higher, something nobler. Aspiring to be a great artist means you desire to touch or enlighten people through your work. Aspiring to be a great football player translates to owning the ability to inspire an audience or a community, to be a role model and a mentor. Ambition combined with a greater purpose will propel you toward success, because you have true motivation.

When you have authentic aspirations, you become self-motivated. This translates into a tangible ability to inspire others. To be a champion, you must become a leader. To be a leader, you must be able to inspire.

CONFIDENCE means understanding both your power and your limitations. Playing to your strengths but ignoring or denying your weaknesses doesn't make you confident, it just makes you **COCKY**. Truly confident people fully investigate their abilities and realize when their talents are needed. What are you truly good at? What do you enjoy doing? What are your assets? Put those things on the table, and be honest with yourself about your shortcomings. Only then will you be able to figure out where you need improvement.

MUSCLE means pushing forward with everything you've got! To complete a power play, you need to rely on the skills and the tools that got you into the game in the first place. With proper preparation and training, your business muscles will be well conditioned and ready for action. How hard are you willing to work to seal the deal? Are you ready to sweat?

Power Play involves the ability to overpower your opponent for the yardage needed. Hired as a junior account executive for New Century Mortgage, I was expected to learn the game fast. Just like playing in the NFL, I only had a limited time to learn the system and make a good first impression. I was given six months to build up my database and learn the fundamentals of closing the deal. Without any prior knowledge of the mortgage banking industry, I had to fall back on what I had learned in the NFL, and I had to trust that those skills would see me through to success. I transformed the office into a football field. I looked at my boss as the head coach, and I placed everyone else in their positions according to their roles in the company. I closely studied the top reps to better understand their tendencies. I wanted to see what they where doing differently that set them apart from the other reps in the office.

The most important thing I noticed was that they had more **AMBITION** and more determination than the other reps in the company. They were also very **CONFIDENT** in their business style, but they were not **COCKY** or arrogant. They understood all the ins and outs of the business. They exuded confidence, and people were drawn to them for it. I also noticed they had a lot of **MUSCLE** around the office when it came to getting things done. Because of the way they handled their clients, their colleagues, and themselves, these reps consistently and successfully orchestrated a **POWER PLAY**.

MAKE YOUR PLAYS...

PLAY ON...

POST GAME REVIEW...

WINS AND LOSSES...

TRAP PLAY

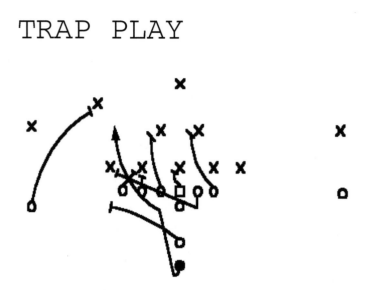

In football, you must create deception on a trap play. You must make your opponent believe something is going to happen in order to control the field. To play this out, you need intent, initiative, and skill.

INTENT. This could very well be the basis for all success. It has to begin here, because without intent, there is no movement, no **MOMENTUM**. You can't become a doctor without first deciding to do so. Super Bowl champions didn't wake up one day wearing the jersey asking themselves how they got there. No. Success begins with intent. The momentum of business, sports, or life can shift or change, but the intent remains. You absolutely have to know what you want before you can go out there and get it. So what do you want? Where are you headed? Tell yourself this: "I *will* be successful. I *will* achieve these goals." If you intend to do something, you must follow through. Achievements don't just "happen" to you. That's a fantasy, not a success story. And by the way, "overnight" successes take years of hard work and dedication. They don't just "happen." You cannot have a purposeful outcome without intent. If you don't know what you want, how will you know when you've attained it?

INITIATIVE is the jump-start that gets the ball moving. In business, like in football, players must **RECOGNIZE OPPORTUNITY** and take the initiative to act on it. A real team player is someone who thinks up cool plays or better ways of doing established tasks. A real asset is someone who takes the ball and runs with it, especially when the other team isn't expecting a new and innovative approach.

SKILL is an asset that sounds like a no-brainer. You must have the skills necessary to play the game. But you'd be surprised how many people think they can play—and win—without first learning the fundamentals. Skills make up the foundation that will sustain you throughout your career, so make sure you understand everything that makes your company work. What do you need to know? Do you need to study? Take a seminar or a workshop? If you realize you might be lacking in an area of your business, don't complain. **EDUCATE** yourself.

Discover your gifts and be thankful for them. Everyone's been blessed with their own skills and strengths. Recognizing your gifts will help you down the right path. My gift was the ability to play football. I believe God gave me this skill, this ability, to put me in the position I'm in today—to help people who might not be able to see past their weaknesses. And the only way to thank God for the gifts I've been given is to use them.

And don't forget to dream big. It all starts with dreams, goals, and objectives. Without these, you have no road map, no plan, no *playbook*. Identify your goals and never lose sight of them. Dreams, like goals, may change into something else, but you must always have them.

On the way to this ranch I said that I wasn't riding any horse. Come on, I'm a kid from the neighborhood... But by the end of the day, things had changed and I did ride a horse. Turned out it was pretty cool. I guess the horse was from the neighborhood too...

MAKE YOUR PLAYS...

PLAY ON...

POST GAME REVIEW...

WINS AND LOSSES...

OPTION PLAY

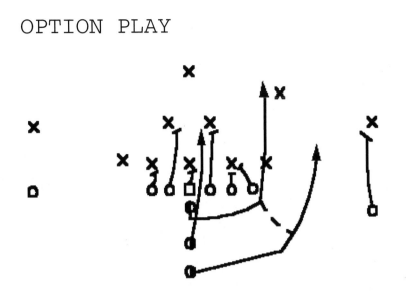

An option play takes advantage of uncertainty on the gridiron. To successfully execute this play, you need flexibility, communication, and a willingness to take risks.

FLEXIBILITY. Every once in a while, you sit back and breathe a sigh of relief because all your accounts are in order, your meetings are lined up, and your presentation promises to be the best you've ever given. Then the corporate climate changes, everything falls apart, and you can't figure out what to do next. You must be able to **ADAPT** to the ever-shifting business world. The game is always moving. The plays are being rewritten. People who succeed understand the nature of change, and they learn to modify their ideas and plans to accommodate the world as it is, not as they would like it to be. Alter your thinking to accept and expect that things will never remain the same. Don't fight it. Embrace change! After all, it's the only thing you can count on.

COMMUNICATION is the cornerstone to a great business structure. This means getting your point across, but it also means paying attention to what the other guy has to say. Listen to your opponents. If you give them the opportunity, they'll tell you everything you need to know to formulate your attack. Always be clear about your objectives for the sake of your teammates, your clients, your boss, and yourself. Never leave anything open to interpretation. Before you leave that meeting, make sure you have established a plan for **FOLLOW-UP**. Are you going to call them? Are they going to call you? When? What were their objections? Will there be another meeting? If so, what needs to be done in the meantime? Businesses are run by people, and no two people are exactly alike in their perception of the world or their ideas about business. You have to try to see the meeting, conference call, or presentation through everyone else's eyes. How did they see the meeting? Did they think it was a success? Were you really as clever as you thought you were?

RISK is key to success. You get nothing out of life if you don't take risks. Now, I'm not recommending you do crazy, stupid, or dangerous things to get you where you want to go. Take risks that are within your established framework of preparation and adaptability you absolutely need to take chances. You need to gamble a little bit. You're familiar with the phrase "Nothing ventured, nothing gained." Now it's time to live it. What are you afraid of? Failure? Everyone has failures in life. A life without failure is a life without gains. Do you really want to live a life that's stagnant and dull? Of course you don't. You want a life that's full of promise, action, and success. You can't have any of that if you don't stick your neck out from time to time. Now, don't forget—risks don't always pay off the way you want them to. But you'll only suffer true failure if you don't recognize the opportunity to learn from your mistakes. Play the "worst case scenario" game with yourself and determine every possible negative outcome. Now, instead of trashing your idea, come up with a game plan for those worst case scenarios. That's right—it all comes back to preparation. No risk is too great if you're prepared for a potential fumble—it just becomes part of your play.

Handshake with former President Bill Clinton.

MAKE YOUR PLAYS...

PLAY ON...

POST GAME REVIEW...

WINS AND LOSSES...

PITCH/SWEEP PLAY

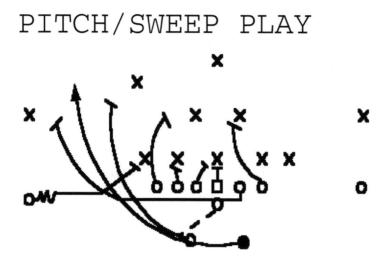

You have to know who to pass the ball to. And you have to know how to follow through. Success in business involves an entire team dedicated to the ultimate goal. If you try to carry the ball all the time, you'll more than likely get cut from the team. In football, sometimes it's best to hand the ball off into someone else's hands. You must know when to let go, how to let go, and to what extent to let go—of a project, a client, a business relationship, a task. What's the best way to get this ball over the goal line?

EXPECTATIONS. Sometimes getting that first meeting is easy, but getting the second meeting is where the real challenge comes into play. Don't walk away from a meeting without first acknowledging the next steps. Did it go well? What was accomplished and what is expected in the future? Deliver the next-step objectives prior to walking out of that meeting, and also learn the answers to the following questions before you leave the meeting: What are the objections? How did they feel about your presentation or your offer? Do they have any questions? And what is the follow-through? Will it be through e-mail messages? Phone calls? Proposals? What's next? Now that you've agreed there will be a next step, you can determine who will do what. You can align your players for the next play. Assign tasks for the players on your team and establish a timetable.

MAKE YOUR PLAYS...

PLAY ON...

POST GAME REVIEW...

WINS AND LOSSES...

SHORT YARDAGE PLAYS

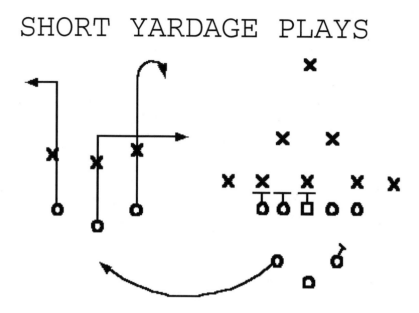

Wealth and success, like football yardage, are gained in increments. This play involves timing, consistency, and patience.

TIMING is everything, they say. And good timing isn't the by-product of luck. A good sense of timing comes from understanding your environment and being ready to manipulate it to your benefit. In a short yardage situation, you need to understand that the main objective is to move the ball a few feet closer to the first-down marker or the goal line. Everything happens in a split second, so every player has to be in position to execute the play. There's no room for hesitation, only execution. In the real world, you must pay attention to your clients, your fellow workers, and your business associates. Understanding their needs will help you make decisions based on what's best for them, not what makes the most sense for you and your timetable.

CONSISTENCY is one key to maintaining focus. To make short yardage plays work, players must be willing to put in the time. They must be **PATIENT** with their progress, because with this type of play, yardage is gained in small increments. In business, sometimes it's better to grind out a desired result instead of rushing things and ending up turning over the ball.

These plays keep the drive alive. When you need to gradually and patiently work a deal, call a short yardage play. When you only need a few more yards or a few more days to close a big deal, call a short yardage play. We can all relate to these types of plays in business or in our personal lives. When I landed my first big account, I called the owner of a large, established company to ask if I could schedule an appointment. I wanted to go over and introduce myself and the company I represented. I really had my sale pitch down to a tee: "New Century Mortgage Corp is the number one sub-prime lender in the industry, and my job is to make sure that your loans fund successfully in a timely manner. I promise I will bust my butt to make sure that you are receiving top-of-the-line service around the clock!" In my mind, I could sell with the best of 'em. I was good! However, no matter how good my pitch sounded, the owner of the company just would not budge. He had a lasting relationship with a competing company and was very pleased with the service he was already getting. He felt there was no need for him to look in any other direction.

I consistently called, asking each time if I could have just a minute or two of his time. I promised it would be worth his while. I wore him down, yard by yard. This went on for a few weeks until he finally agreed to see me. The rep from the competing company dropped the ball, and I seized the opportunity. I was there waiting for it. I gained yardage by being

CONSISTENT, taking advantage of **TIMING**, and being **PATIENT**. We closed the deal, and he turned over all his business to me. My book of business went from zero to millions overnight.

MAKE YOUR PLAYS...

PLAY ON...

POST GAME REVIEW...

WINS AND LOSSES...

MID TO LONG YARDAGE PLAYS

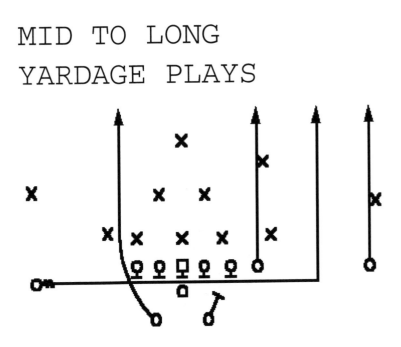

Long yardage passes are typically harder to complete, but when they're successful, the benefits are huge. This is where you really have to trust your teammates enough to risk putting it all on the line and letting it fly. This is where you can change the momentum of the game.

RISK is something we all have to entertain to succeed in life. In a long-yardage play, you have to make sure all your players are in position and everyone knows exactly what's expected of them. This is not a solo risk that puts your individual ego on the line. This is a collective risk, shared by the whole team. In this scenario, you must work together as a well-oiled machine. If all the elements of the play are executed with precision, a successful completion can change the entire **MOMENTUM** of the game. Unfortunately, an interception can do the same thing, but in a very negative way. Be prepared for all outcomes to make sure the risk is worth taking. Gather as much information as you can, and make sure all of your team members are on board before you throw that ball.

Taking this type of risk involves placing a great deal of **TRUST** in your teammates. Sometimes that's hard to do. You think you can manage on your own because you're afraid others won't pull their own weight. It's easy to fall into the habit of doing it all yourself to get it done right. But that's not always possible in business. You must relinquish control and be content to complete only the task that has been assigned to you. Your teammates will pick up the slack; that's what they're there for. With everyone doing their part, greater goals can be achieved easier and quicker.

MAKE YOUR PLAYS...

PLAY ON...

POST GAME REVIEW...

WINS AND LOSSES...

HAIL MARY PASS

This play works best when you have nothing left but your **DREAMS** and your **FAITH**. If you have prepared yourself for the game through training, education, and exercise, the Hail Mary is not as desperate as it might seem. If you need to get out of a tight spot and you fully understand your game, you will be blessed with superior insight and pointed toward a better solution. When you feel like you have nothing to lose, take your best shot and let the ball fly. If nothing else, you will switch up the momentum and move the game in a different direction.

Plays are called every day, both in our personal lives and in our business lives. The question is whether you're ready to take full advantage of your opportunity to display your talents. I can remember many times in my life when I needed a play that would get me through the day. One time in my life that really sticks out was when I found myself anxiously waiting by the phone to see whether all the years of blood, sweat, and tears would finally pay off. It was the second day of the 1996 NFL draft. Already out of position, as a 205-pound linebacker for a team that finished 3–8, I would need a miracle. I needed a **HAIL MARY PASS**, a play that relied on my **DREAMS** and **FAITH**. With the most important decision of my football career looming, I realized at that moment, waiting by the phone, that I had no control over what the outcome would be.

Nothing about the year leading up to the draft went as planned. As a starter for one of the most dominating defenses for the past three years in the Pac-10, it was finally my time to shine. I remember going to the defensive coordinator and asking if I could get some playing time at the safety position. I knew that position would be more realistic for me at the next level. The coach told me no. He felt I would best help the team as a linebacker. Then, in addition to playing out of position, one of our pre-season All-American defense linemen had a severe case of "turf-toe" and would miss half of the season. For us to have any chance, we really needed Baby Shaq to be out there clogging up the middle and creating havoc on opposing quarterbacks. The more games you win, the more national attention you get, plain and simple. Unfortunately, that was not the case for us. We could not buy a win that year.

The season ended with no one beating down my door; no one asking me for a private workout with their club. There were no letters from any of the all-star committees asking, "Would you like to play in our bowl game?" It was just me, my girl, my baby boy, and my trainer Dr. Hart. I knew that at least they believed in me. I trained for hours and hours every day. I did not attend class that last semester, so I could focus on preparing for the workouts at the school. I figured I could always come back and go to school, but I would never have another chance to play in the NFL. Certain players were invited to Indy to work out at the combine. The combine happens every year before the draft. It's where players can raise their stock and secure a higher place in the draft. This, of course, leads to a bigger payday or secures them a roster spot on someone's team. However, for me, it boiled down to checking the schedule to see when the scouts would be there to workout the pre-season All-American. I had to piggyback off Baby Shaq's name. But that's okay. In life, we all need other people to get to where we trying to go, right?

Game Time. With my family at my side, it was time to make it happen. Looking at my baby and picturing my baby's face before lining up to run that 40 yard dash, made me dig deep down inside and pull out all I had. With no plan B established, there was no turning back: it was all or nothing. This was my shot to show everyone in the building that I could play on the next level. They said I was neither fast enough, nor big enough to play in the NFL. But they did not know me, did not know what I had been through to get there. It was pure heart and determination. No one but God knows a man's heart and only a man knows what he is willing to do to get what he wants. I became a man possessed.

The first time I ran the 40, I was clocked at a 4.45. The tone was set; all the hard work was finally paying off. I heard one of the scouts ask, "Who is that?" Then another scout said, "That's Chris Hayes, the undersized linebacker that might be a tweener." A "tweener" is someone who is in between two different positions. For me, it meant that I was as an undersized linebacker, who may be able to play safety in the league. It was not unheard of. There had been players to do it before me, and some of those players went on to have Hall of Fame careers. However, there still were no guarantees. I was actually being worked out as a safety, the position I had asked my coach to switch me to. Although I had never played the position on the collegiate level, I performed well in the drills, and the scout from the New York Jets took an interest in me.

Mr. Marv Sutherland was the scout in our local area. Marv asked me several question in regard to playing safety in the NFL. I told him that it didn't matter where I played. If given the chance, I would play wherever the coach wanted me to play. Marv asked me to do some defensive back drills while being video taped. That was the last I heard from Marv until after the draft. The anticipation of the draft was unbearable. I waited anxiously, hoping and praying. I knew that I had done everything in my power to play the game the best I knew how. The rest was left to faith. I was not drafted on the first day, but I did get a call from the New York Jets the following day, as their first pick in the seventh round. I could have easily given up and believed all the doubters. But I chose to persevere and fight for my dreams.

MAKE YOUR PLAYS...

PLAY ON...

POST GAME REVIEW...

WINS AND LOSSES...

DEFENSIVE FORMATIONS

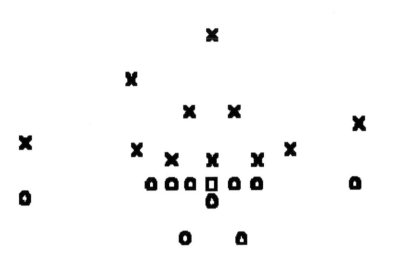

In life, as in football, sometimes you're on defense. A good defense means being able to anticipate an outcome and react to any situation. Understanding your opponent and being able to predict which way he or she might go is fundamental to preventing an unfavorable situation for yourself or your business. Research your game plan and see each play through the eyes of the other side.

PERCEPTION. This is where you must put yourself in the other guy's shoes. Understand the company you're dealing with. Investigate each individual player and their perception of the situation, the job, the deal. This is how you anticipate the play.

Researching the background of a potential business partner is a powerful tool, but most people don't take the time to use the many **RESOURCES** available to them. We have many resources at our disposal. For example, do a simple Internet search on them. Find out what charities they're involved in. Are they married? Do they have children? Look at their past projects and insert accolades into your negotiations. Do it in a way that lets them know you're interested in them as a person. Always try to maintain some level of personal connection.

No matter which side you're on, in order to play the game effectively and ultimately win, you must **DREAM**. Just the fact you picked up this playbook proves that you have dreams. Dream big. It all starts with dreams, goals, and objectives. Without these, you have no roadmap, no plan, no *playbook*. Identify your goals and never lose sight of them.

Hard work comes next—that's playing the game. Remember: no one is entitled to anything, only those who put in the hours get the rewards. Putting in the hours means you're committed and enthusiastic. Now go **WIN** that game!

MAKE YOUR PLAYS...

PLAY ON...

POST GAME REVIEW...

WINS AND LOSSES...

Post Game Review:

Now with another game or big deal under your belt, it's time to recap your overall performance. Now you'll have the opportunity to break down each play to see whether you executed according to your game plan. In this game called life, it's very important that you're honest with yourself. Look in the mirror and ask, "Am I being all I can be?" In football and in life, tomorrow is not guaranteed. You have to take full advantage of your opportunities. You have to be willing to leave it all on the field. Victory is won through sacrifice. What are you willing to sacrifice to be the best? How many extra hours will you commit to, how long after work will you stay to master your craft? Everyone gets excited watching their favorite athlete score the game winning touchdown or the game winning shot. But do you really know what's required to get to that point? Maybe you need to run extra routes after practice or shoot 3,000 free-throws when no one else is in the building. The truth is: There is no secret or magic potion you can take to be the best. It involves recognizing your strengths and weaknesses and applying the tools you've been given in this lifetime.

I believe that each and every one of us has a special gift from God to allow us to unlock that champion within. The reason why I'm able to achieve success is because I'm always gearing up for the big game. Suits on, Game on. Know your position—it's all about having a winning attitude and the determination to persevere. It's the mentality of a warrior putting on armor for battle. Gladiator's of the green, the strongest of the fittest. Who wants it more? You? Or the other guy? You must become the type of player who always shows up to play. The "go-to" guy. When the game is on the line, they count on you to bring it home. You have to pay the cost to be the boss. We have all heard that before. There is a price that has to be paid every time you climb up the corporate ladder. To whom much is given, much is required. Are you a team player? Do you have the team's overall goals and objectives in mind? What type of boss are you? Are you the type of coach who cares about his or her own selfish desires? Are you the type of coach who tries to do everyone else's job? There is a reason why corporations keep more than one person at the controls. There has to be someone to keep you accountable for your actions.

Not only do you have to know your position on the field; you have to know how to play your position. Playmakers are players that get excited when presented with a challenge. By being fundamentally sound in everything you do, and by focusing on the small things that make you great, you will be able to take your game to the next level. Coaches always tell you to leave your personal life off the field. We all have problems; some more than others. But when you step on the field or in the office, there should be only one thing on your mind— win the game.

SOME FINAL WORDS FROM CHRIS:

In closing, I hope I was able to relate to you the basic principles of the powerful message of self-confidence and positioning. I believe that every one of us is equipped with the necessary tools we need to compete in the game of life. It's simple. First, you must understand the rules of the game; then you must execute. Most things in life have to be earned. I was fortunate enough to run through that tunnel onto that football field for eight years of my life. But it wasn't free. I had to pay the price. I chose to believe in myself and to rely on the people I trusted to motivate and inspire me. You have to dig deep inside yourself and ask, "What type of player am I?" Once you understand the game, and your place in it, pick up your play book. Study the plays, the strategies, the tactics, so that you'll be prepared to play the game at the highest level.

I am who I say I am.
I am a child of The Most High.
I am a Champion.

I am a loving husband to my wife Aran.
I am a proud father of three sons.
And I love serving people and giving back.

You must constantly reaffirm your commitment to WHO YOU ARE and what you represent. So get off the bench and get in the game, THE GAME OF LIFE!

Peace,

Chris "Peto" Hayes

"Suits On, Game On" is just the beginning…
Look for my next book:
I Ain't Playing, "To Whom Much Is Given, Much Is Required"

This book is a unique description of football that captures the true-life perspective of the game from my experiences in the NFL. I will take you on my journey from the rough West Side of San Bernardino, California, to college in Washington State, to getting drafted and playing football in the NFL. This is my life's testimony on the trials and tribulations that we all face. I believe we all have been equipped with the necessary tools to succeed in life. I also believe that too many people of influence self-destruct before they have the opportunity to give back. Sadly, this is due to their lack of self-knowledge, their failure to understand the significance of their gifts, or their unwillingness to realize their true purpose. To whom much is given, much is required, is the premise upon which one must build. It is truly a blessing to have knowledge in life, but knowing how to apply this knowledge is just as important. My years in the NFL were just a fraction of my life. It took me years to realize there is so much more. I once heard that opportunities of a lifetime must be seized in the lifetime of the opportunity. This means that you have to take advantage of what life has to offer and make the best out of it right there in the moment. I had to learn my purpose the hard way, before my gifts were taken away. It happened for me in a hospital emergency room holding my chest and gasping for air...

But I'm one of the lucky ones. I got a second chance in life. This book will unlock the champion within, and show you how to realize and take advantage of the gifts that were bestowed upon you.

Chris Hayes' Biography:

Following graduation from Washington State University, Mr. Hayes was drafted by the New York Jets in the seventh round (210th overall) of the 1996 NFL draft. He was waived by the Jets at the end of training camp in August, 1996, and signed onto the Washington Redskins practice squad that September. After being waived by the Redskins on October 1, 1996, Mr. Hayes was immediately signed to the Green Bay Packers practice squad. Mr. Hayes was traded to the Jets in June, 1997, re-signed with the Jets in March, 1998, and was later signed to the Packers active roster in December, 1998. After being released by the New York Jets on February 25, 2002, Mr. Hayes was signed by the Patriots as a veteran free agent on March 12, 2002. He retired from the NFL following the 2004 season.

Mr. Hayes played in all three of Green Bay's postseason games in 1996, including Super Bowl XXXI against the Patriots.

Chris Hayes has established C I J Chris Hayes, Inc. (more popularly known as 30THIRTY HAYES) -- a faith-based non-profit foundation that provides community services to youth and young adults. The foundation, which derives its name from the first initials of his three sons, Christopher, Isaiah, and Jeremiah, provides educational training programs, job training/placement programs, motivational speaking, community outreach services and football coaching for youth.

Eight-year National Football League veteran and Super Bowl XXXI champion Chris Hayes created *30THIRTY HAYES* in response to his heart's cry to facilitate change in the youth of his hometown.

Chris was born on May 7, 1972, in San Bernardino, California. He has worked with troubled teenagers throughout his college and NFL career, and has intensified his outreach efforts since retiring from the NFL. He frequently visits detention centers and county jails to counsel troubled youth and incarcerated convicts. Chris credits the time he spent in the Fairfax (CA) Continuation School as the major turning point in his life after he was expelled from high school as a sophomore. Chris recognizes his high school coach, Carl Guyton, and his continuation teacher, Dean Nord, as two of the most positive influences in his life.

In high school, Chris was voted team MVP, all-conference and All-Los Angeles as a defensive back. He also lettered in basketball at San Gorgonio (San Bernardino, California) High School.

Chris and his wife, Aran, have three sons Christopher, Jr., Isaiah, and Jeremiah.

MORE BOOKS COMING SOON FROM:

I AIN'T PLAYING:
To Whom Much Is Given, Much Is Required
By Chris Hayes

THE LEON BENDER STORY
By Derek Sparks

LESSONS OF THE GAME: Part II
The Collegiate Version
By Derek Sparks